Inspiring Thoughts

Joyful Possibilities
to Color and Display

ZENDOODLE COLORSCAPES: INSPIRING THOUGHTS.
Copyright © 2020 by St. Martin's Press. All rights reserved.
Printed in Canada. For information, address
St. Martin's Press, 120 Broadway, New York, NY 10271.

www.castlepointbooks.com

The Castle Point Books trademark is owned by Castle Point Publishing, LLC.
Castle Point books are published and distributed by St. Martin's Publishing Group.

ISBN 978-1-250-27109-9 (trade paperback)

Our books may be purchased in bulk for promotional, educational, or business use.
Please contact your local bookseller or the Macmillan Corporate and Premium
Sales Department at 1-800-221-7945, extension 5442, or by email
at MacmillanSpecialMarkets@macmillan.com.

First Edition: 2020

10 9 8 7 6 5 4 3 2 1

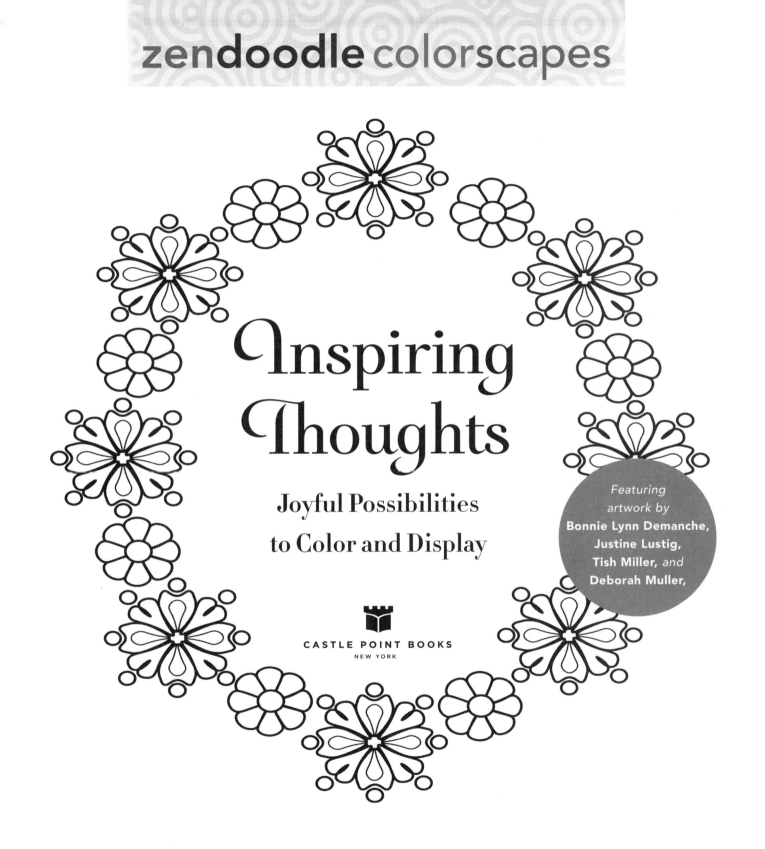

zendoodle colorscapes

Inspiring Thoughts

Joyful Possibilities to Color and Display

CASTLE POINT BOOKS
NEW YORK

Featuring artwork by **Bonnie Lynn Demanche, Justine Lustig, Tish Miller,** and **Deborah Muller,**

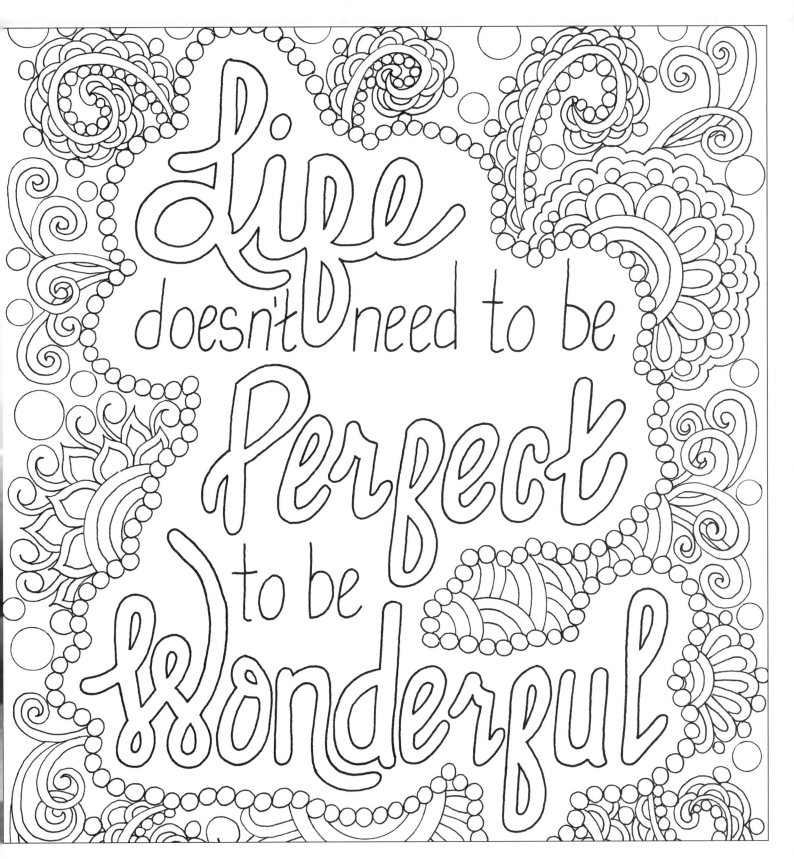

...and they lived happily ever after

LIFE
is all about
creating yourself

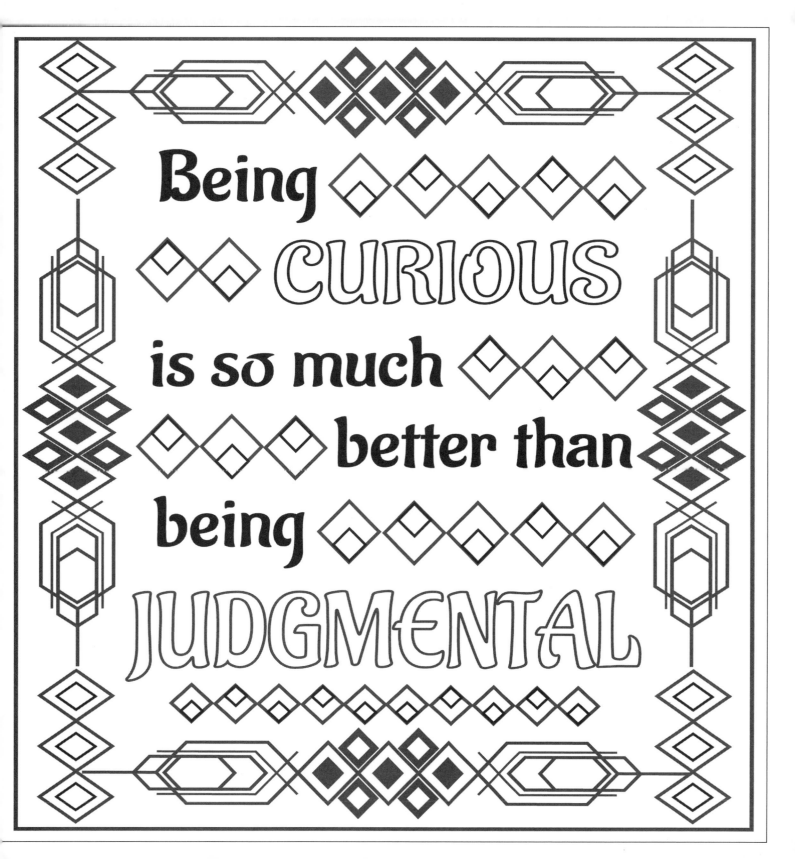

Being CURIOUS is so much better than being JUDGMENTAL